P9-DME-054

Parrots

Debbie Gallagher

Marshall Cavendish
Benchmark
New York

This edition first published in 2010 in the United States of America by Marshall Cavendish Benchmark
An imprint of Marshall Cavendish Corporation

All rights reserved.

No part of this publication may be reproduced, stored in a retrieval system or transmitted, in any form or by any means, electronic, mechanical, photocopying, recording, or otherwise, without the prior permission of the copyright owner. Request for permission should be addressed to the Publisher, Marshall Cavendish Corporation, 99 White Plains Road, Tarrytown, NY 10591. Tel: (914) 332-8888, fax: (914) 332-1888.

Website: www.marshallcavendish.us

This publication represents the opinions and views of the author based on Debbie Gallagher's personal experience, knowledge, and research. The information in this book serves as a general guide only. The author and publisher have used their best efforts in preparing this book and disclaim liability rising directly and indirectly from the use and application of this book.

Other Marshall Cavendish Offices:
Marshall Cavendish Ltd. 5th Floor, 32-38 Saffron Hill, London EC1N 8 FH, UK • Marshall Cavendish International (Asia) Private Limited, 1 New Industrial Road, Singapore 536196 • Marshall Cavendish International (Thailand) Co Ltd. 253 Asoke, 12th Flr, Sukhumvit 21 Road, Klongtoey Nua, Wattana, Bangkok 10110, Thailand • Marshall Cavendish (Malaysia) Sdn Bhd, Times Subang, Lot 46, Subang Hi-Tech Industrial Park, Batu Tiga, 40000 Shah Alam, Selangor Darul Ehsan, Malaysia

Marshall Cavendish is a trademark of Times Publishing Limited

All websites were available and accurate when this book was sent to press.

Contents

When a word is printed in **bold**, you can look up its meaning in the Glossary on page 31.

Zoos

Zoos are places where people can see a lot of different animals. The animals in a zoo come from all around the world.

People can visit zoos to see animals from other parts of the world.

Zoos have special **enclosures** for each different type of animal. Some enclosures are like the animals' homes in the **wild**. They have trees for climbing and water for swimming.

Animals such as birds and monkeys need enclosures with high roofs and many trees.

Parrots

Parrots are a type of bird that lives in trees. Parrots have strong legs and claws on their feet that can hold things tightly. They have short, curved **bills**.

curved bill

strong, bright colors

two claws pointing forward

Macaws are the largest parrots in the world.

There are more than three hundred and fifty **species** of parrot. Many parrots are green, but parrots can be all sorts of colors. Some parrots are mostly white or mostly black.

A sulfur-crested cockatoo is mostly white, with a yellow crest of feathers on its head.

In the Wild

In the wild, parrots live in warm areas of the world. They live in forest **habitats** where they spend most of their time high up in the trees.

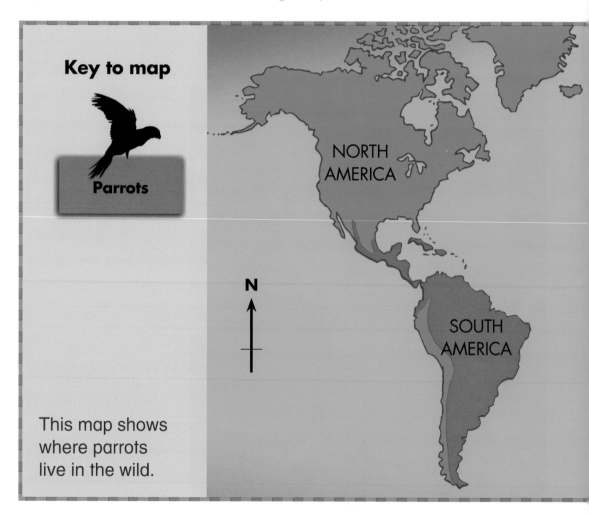

Key to map

Parrots

This map shows where parrots live in the wild.

NORTH AMERICA

N

SOUTH AMERICA

Parrots live in families or groups, called flocks.
Most male and female adult parrots form pairs.
Each pair stays together for life.

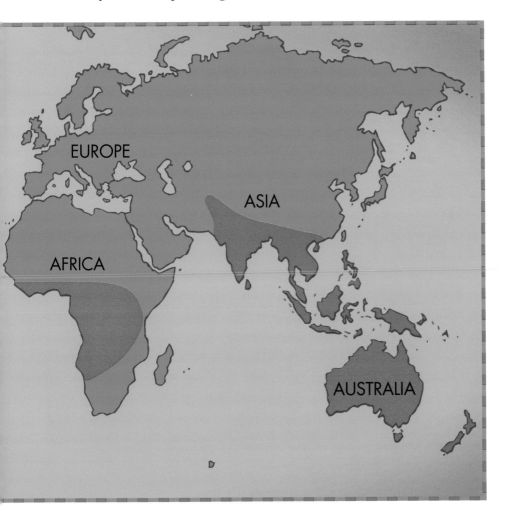

Threats to Survival

One threat to the survival of parrots comes from **poachers**. Poachers go into the natural habitats of parrots and capture the birds or their eggs.

Capturing parrots threatens their survival in the wild.

Poachers sell the parrots as pets. Parrots are popular pets. People like their interesting colors and the way some parrots can copy human sounds.

Parrots are sometimes kept in cages as pets.

Zoo Homes

In zoos, parrots live in enclosures called aviaries. Aviaries are large enough for parrots to fly around. Many zoos create aviaries that are like the parrots' habitats in the wild.

cage

ropes

trees

Different species of parrot may live in the same large aviary.

Parrot aviaries should have trees. The trees should have different types of branches for chewing, **perching,** and climbing.

Parrots perch on branches to eat and rest.

Zoo Food

Parrots eat fruit, seeds, and nuts. Some parrots eat nectar, which is a type of honey found in flowers. Other parrots eat insects.

A parrot's zoo food includes fruit, seeds, and nuts.

A Parrot's Zoo Food
fruit
seeds
nuts
nectar
insects

Feeding

Zookeepers are careful to feed parrots the right amounts of the right foods. Parrots **forage** for food. Zookeepers hide food so that parrots have to look for it.

Macaws gather to eat zoo food.

Zoo Health

Zookeepers weigh the parrots to make sure they are healthy. The zookeepers need to check that the parrots are getting the right amount of food.

A zookeeper weighs a parrot.

Zookeepers record how the parrots behave, especially if the birds do something different. They write down what the birds eat and anything unusual that happens during the day.

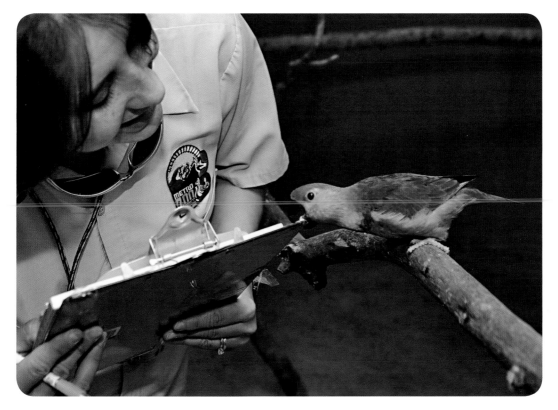

A zookeeper checks for any unusual behavior.

Baby Parrots

Baby parrots, called chicks, come from eggs. Mother parrots lay the eggs. Some lay their eggs in holes in trees. Some dig holes in cliffs or build nests from sticks.

Some parrots build their nests in holes in trees.

Chicks have no feathers when they hatch. Both parents feed the chicks. Chicks stay in the nest for up to four months.

Sometimes, a zookeeper needs to take care of newborn parrots.

How Zoos Are Saving Parrots

Many species of parrot are **endangered**. Some zoos help save parrots by **breeding** endangered birds. Some zoos collect money to protect parrot habitats or take in injured or abandoned parrots.

Visitors to zoos help raise money to save parrots.

Auckland Zoo, in New Zealand, is helping save the kakapo. There are about ninety kakapo left in the wild. Zoo **veterinarians** go into the wild to check the birds are healthy.

A zoo vet checks a kakapo in the wild.

Zoos Working Together

Zoos work together to breed parrot species that no longer live in the wild. There are no Spix's macaws left in the wild, but some are kept in zoos.

Zoos work together to breed Spix's macaws.

Zoos share and swap birds so they can breed.
If zoos breed large numbers of endangered
parrots, some can be returned to the wild.

Some parrots
born in zoos are
released into
the wild.

Meet Thomas, a Parrot Keeper

Thomas works as a zookeeper, caring for parrots.

Question	Why did you become a zookeeper?
Answer	I did work experience with a zoo during high school and loved it.
Question	How long have you been a zookeeper?
Answer	I have been a zookeeper for nine years.

Thomas prepares food for the parrots.

Question	What animals have you worked with?
Answer	I have worked with eagles, parrots, elephants, wolves, and **reptiles**.
Question	What do you like about your job?
Answer	I love those special moments when a parrot decides to come to you to make contact.

A Day in the Life of a Zookeeper

Zookeepers have jobs to do every day. Often, a team of zookeepers work together to look after the birds at a zoo.

7:30 a.m.
Prepare food for the parrots.

8:30 a.m.
Rake the pathway in the aviary before visitors arrive.

11:30 a.m.

Check the health of parrots that have arrived recently.

4:00 p.m.

Write in the Parrots' Daily Report about any changes in a parrot's behavior or what it is eating.

Zoos Around the World

There are zoos all around the world. Jurong Bird Park, in Singapore, has the world's largest walk-in bird aviary. Its Parrot Paradise exhibit holds fifty-two different species of parrot.

Visitor walkways are at treetop level in the Jurong Bird Park.

The zookeepers at Jurong Bird Park have made aviaries that are like the birds' natural habitats. The South-East Asia aviary has machines that spray their birds so that it is like light rain in the wild.

The macaws have lots of things to climb and perch on, like in the wild.

The Importance of Zoos

Zoos do very important work. They:

- help people learn about animals
- save endangered animals and animals that are badly treated

Bali Bird Park in Indonesia is breeding the endangered Pesquet's parrot.

Glossary

bills   Beaks.

breeding   Caring for animals so that they can produce babies.

enclosures   The fenced-in areas where animals are kept in zoos.

endangered   At high risk of dying out and disappearing from Earth.

forage   To wander around searching for food.

habitats   Areas in which animals are naturally found.

perching   Resting or coming to land on something.

poachers   People who hunt or capture animals illegally.

reptiles   A group of animals, such as snakes and crocodiles, with dry, scaly skin.

species   Groups of animals or plants that have similar features.

veterinarians Animal doctors.

wild   Natural areas, such as forests, that are untouched by humans.

Index